Don't Get Lost in the Fog!

Learning, Living, and Life

Life and Business Lessons Learned While Catfishing on the

Tennessee River

Contents

What Makes Up a Trotline

Before we get to stories and lessons, I should discuss and explain some of the tools, techniques, and rules of catfishing. Understanding how a trotline is constructed and catfishing is performed will help us understand and appreciate the metaphor of fishing and life.

Our trotlines consisted of 100 hooks. A nylon main line would be approximately 375 feet in length. A trotline is considered the entire line, hooks, floats, and anchors ready to catch fish. We built the lines on shore or in the water. One end of the line was tied to an anchor heavy enough to hold the entire line in place against river currents and the pulling of the boat against winds as one would be "running" the line.

The anchor consisted of wheel rims or two or three concrete blocks. From the end anchor the main line would begin without hooks for 10 to 15 yards. Then a leader line for

a jug or float would be added. A float or jug leader line would

be at each end of the trotline, and all the fishing would take

place between these two main float leader lines. Three feet

after the floater line, you would place the first hook leader

line. These lines would be two feet in length and placed three

feet apart. At the bottom of the hook leader line, a swivel

and hook would be tied.

In later years, we placed the swivel on the top of the

hook leader line where it connected to the main line. The

swivel kept the hook leader line from twisting around the

main line due to changing current and when a fish was

caught. Periodically, as you added the hook leader lines to

the main line, you would add an additional float line or a long

thin leader line to place a small anchor. The float between

the two main end floats along with the smaller anchor leader would allow the line to be a different distance from the river

bottom. One could easily add or remove floats or anchors

depending if the fish were biting best in deep water or closer

to the surface.

Lesson 1

Mom was raised in the nearby city of Harriman in Roane County and moved south of the river to the lake in the late 50s. That is where my three siblings and I were born. Brice is the oldest; I was second-born, followed by my two younger brothers, Randall and Preston. We never all fished together as the two younger brothers began after Brice and I began our adult lives and careers. We fished during the late spring, summer, and early fall of each year. The two denominators that held us together were Mom and Dad.

We catfished on the Tennessee River Watts Bar Lake Reservoir. This is the story of our adventures and many of the lessons of life and business we learned from our catfishing experiences. Dad was born in the south of the river area of Roane County, Tennessee, and fished, as a young boy, with his uncles, Fred and Charlie Keylon. As I write this book, Dad is eighty and would admit that he is still learning tricks of the fishing trade to this day.

The first lesson to learn here is to always be open-minded to learning.

Lesson 2

Image how a trotline looks in the river. One can see that a trotline from beginning of the anchor to the end can depict life from the bottom of the river or dust of the earth. We start our lives, and the journey has ups and downs along the way until life ends, and we return to dust or the bottom of the river. We hope life gives us more ups than downs, but we must realize and recognize that there will be ups and downs. But life goes on, and you should keep on fishing and living life.

So here we have lesson two: life has its ups and downs.

Lesson 3

To be successful in fishing as in life, you must equip yourself with the correct tools. Lesson three is to have the right tools such as an equipped boat and a fully functioning trotline. We will discuss the particular aspects of these and other tools later. For now we have a trotline and a boat. The Woody boys had as many as thirteen lines with 100 hooks each, which meant fishing was hard work.

Now let us begin the journey of many more lessons learned catfishing on the Tennessee River.

Take Time to Sharpen the Hooks/Knives

A fish may not be caught unless the hooks are sharp.

One must take time to sharpen one's skills.

Fishing is like life, business, family, school, or in anything you do. You must keep your hooks and skills sharp. Be your best; bring your best to the game. To be successful at fishing, we must have sharp hooks. The fish are hard enough to catch, so why make your task any harder? If you want to make the sale, you want to sell yourself, put on your best.

One of our greatest weaknesses in fishing was we did not sharpen or replace our hooks often enough, a lesson we learned later when we went from galvanized hooks to stainless steel hooks. Stainless steel hooks were a little smaller and harder to put on a swivel without breaking, but the result was far superior. The stainless steel hooks were sharper and remained sharp. Yes, fishing improved by sharpening our tools. One could call it improvement or advancement in technology. One might think fishing would not change much over the years, but there were skills to learn about fishing then and still today. Continue to sharpen your skills. Sharpening your skills is what keeps you a step ahead of your competition.

I graduated from college in 1983 when computers were first making an impact in office automation with word processing and spreadsheets. After a quarter break from school, it was time to go back to college and learn word processing and Lotus 123 —or was it Super Cal, or maybe both? I had learned over time you don't stand still or the crowd will pass you by. You must keep learning and growing;

the next generation is after your fish or your job. Stay ahead of the new fisherman. Keep your eyes open, your mind open and continue to grow and learn by sharpening your hooks and, of course, your knives and personal skills.

Speaking of knives, Dad always says a dull knife will cut you more than a sharp knife. I agree; I witnessed it. With a dull knife, you must put more energy into the cut and thus are subject to making more mistakes. Every time before we cleaned fish, Dad would sharpen the knives. The cut was cleaner, finer, smoother, and more precise and therefore required less energy. Requiring less energy meant we were more productive.

> *"Give me six hours to chop down a tree and I will spend the first four sharpening the axe."* Abraham Lincoln

Taking the time to sharpen your skills will make life easier, safer, and you will be more productive. I want to hire the individual with not only the sharpest skills but the one with the initiative to keep them sharp. The whetstone stayed on the cleaning table always ready for the next catch of the day.

What to do With a Hung or Tangled Line

Lines get tangled up just like life. You can spend time untangling, but sometimes you must cut the lines and restart your place in the line or in life.

The trotline is a long 100-hook nylon green or white line that would run from one anchor and float to another float and anchor, a span of some 300 feet. The line would often run across the channel and the water's current would pull the line along the bottom. Often the debris on the bottom of the river would hang up the line. What do you do with a hung line penned to the bottom of the river? Sometimes a hard pull would cause the line to release. Sometimes the line would remain hung but would slip and then tighten back up, pulling and pushing up and down like a seesaw, but never releasing.

What did we do? We learned patience. We might drop the line and go to the float on the other end of where the line was hung and run the line in the opposite direction back to the hung line point, hoping the line would release.

A hung line is similar to working with employees who may not be doing what is needed for the organization. You work with them, you try to salvage the investment in the line, the employee. If the line did not release, we would drop the line and come back later hoping the river current would release the line overnight. We were patient and gave the line another chance hoping the time away would resolve the problem. Many times working the line or letting the line rest was successful. Sometimes work and time would not release the line, and our problem could not be solved and the line became unproductive. When this happened, it was time to bring out the sharp knives and cut our losses. Like an unproductive employee, sometimes, it is best to cut the losses (maybe we should say losers) and start again. A man once said to me, "We hire people based on skill and knowledge, and let them go based on chemistry." Folks in your organization must get along, and if they don't, sometimes you must cut the line, letting the taut end of the line go away. We then would get a second boat to bring the two now slack ends together and retie the line. Heal the organization of the bad chemistry.

Try to fix your problem people, but after a while if you are unsuccessful, you must cut your losses. Replace the bad chemistry with good chemistry and create another successful trotline. What is the old saying? "It is not the people you fire that cause you problems; it is the people you

don't." *Sometimes you must cut the line that is hung.*

Tangled lines operate on the same principle. Start

with patience and time, and if they fail then you cut your

tangled line and move on.

Trotline Too Taut

Too taut a line and your fish can get off.

Too many Rules – One cannot do his/her job if we are constantly worrying about breaking the rules.

A trotline needs to have enough slack so we can catch the fish. An organization needs to have enough slack to change as the economic market changes and culture changes.

It's important to know how taut or slack the trotline needs to be. A trotline is anchored at each end with weights to hold the line in position. The distance between the anchors and the depth of the water determines how taut or slack the line will be. A line that is too taut will allow the hooked fish to swim and pull the hook out of his mouth. A line too slack is more prone to become tangled or hung up on debris on the bottom of the river. The rules of being too rigid or too lax applies to how we manage an organization and to how we raise our families.

Consider the trotline as rules of an organization. Too taut a line or too restrictive rules create a negative atmosphere that could limit how productive, explorative, experimental, and creative our organization can be. Rules that are too slack could also cause organizations to appear not responsible or unfocused on a common mission. Employees could be in a position of not understanding or knowing their boundaries. Rules that are too restrictive could cause decisions to be made by top management, when they should be, and could be, made by lower management, thus taking important time away from a visionary leader. Top management is unable to focus on the organization's mission, goals and direction as they have forced themselves

20

to spend valuable time on routine decisions. If rules and directions are too loose, an organization can fail to reach its goals.

Too restrictive, too tight, and too loose or relaxed rules are one of the most difficult decisions management must make. It's what I call "Balanced Management." Depending on the type of organization or business also dictates where the "Balance" would fall on the spectrum. An accounting organization would probably have more stringent rules than a marketing firm. An engineering firm would need to be both restrictive and relaxed. Rules of its organization help to establish the culture.

Raising children appears to have the same attributes. Some children need more relaxed rules than others. My older brother needed more rules. I, on the other hand, saw the

21

ways of my older brother and his punishment and learned a

lesson from some of his mistakes.

Back to fishing: Too taut a trotline, and the fish will

get off the line, and too slack, the fish will take the line under

debris and hang your line. Be cautious in managing and

raising children. Each individual is different and needs special

care and attention. Find your sweet spot and manage your

"Balance." *Be willing to change as you run the line across the*

river of life.

Identify What You Need

Make a list of what is needed to achieve a goal.

- Paddles —safety backup plan -A tool of risk management

- Boat —essential tool of productivity

- Motor —tool of efficiency

- Water plug —a tool of risk management

- Life vest —a tool of risk management

- Knives, hooks, buckets —some are necessities and some improve productivity

- Clothes —a tool of risk management and to improve effectiveness for the morning and evening of fishing (hats, long sleeves, long pants)

As you go through your private life or business, you must take an inventory of what you have and what you need to accomplish your desired task and meet your goals. Make a list of what you need either mentally or, even better, write it down. In fishing you a need a boat in which you travel. It does not need to be the most expensive nor be equipped with all the modern fishing gadgets. It only needs to be able to get the job done. We had two 14 foot Jon boats equipped with either a 6 or 10 horsepower Johnson motor. They were not the fastest boats and motors, but they were sufficient. They got the job done and that job was to get from the shore to each line and back to the shore again, hopefully with a load of fish.

Determine what you need to get the job done. However, have a backup plan just in case something happens to the motor; yes, that's a paddle. The paddle helps you manage your risk of being broken down without a way to get home. In life and in business, manage your risk and understand what your risk may be. You don't need two motors, which is overkill and expensive, when a $10 paddle is enough to manage your risk. Understand and identify what could go wrong and then determine what you need to alleviate the risk.

This reminds me of a situation that happened while a friend was fishing with me one summer. Alan Owen, my good friend, always was talking about fishing and he loved catfishing and trotline fishing for the blue and channel cats. Well, I was out of college and moved back with my mom and dad for the summer. When Mom and Dad left for a week in Florida, I called Alan and asked if he wanted to fish Dad's lines that week. Alan, a local newspaper journalist who had run a full page article on Dad about catfishing, was all in. I baited the lines one evening and asked Alan to join me after work the next day to see if we had any big cats. It was a

Wednesday evening in mid-summer 1983. In case you may not know, in the summer of 1983 in mid-week, there were to our knowledge no other boats on the lake at around 7:00 p.m. Alan and I caught a tub full of fish on the first two lines and as we traveled to the third, well you guessed it, the motor quit. I tried and tried to restart the motor with no luck. I told Alan we had to paddle home. Yes, we had two paddles, but my good friend Alan kept to his promise he had made years earlier that he would never paddle. Maybe this should be a lesson about the kind of friends we should have? Anyway, I paddled and paddled but within a few minutes we saw a lone bass boat on Watts Bar Lake coming in for the evening. I flagged him down, and he graciously towed us in. We had a boat load of fish and a broken motor. Lesson learned: *sometimes your friends won't paddle.*

As we were being towed in I thought, "I'm being repaid for the times Dad, my brothers, and I helped others who broke down over the years." Help others succeed and one day someone will help you. I still have a friend in Alan except when it comes to paddling the boat —that's something I know he will never do.

Everything can be set up just right and the fish may still not bite.

Everything may be aligned for success but success may not come today; one must persevere.

Yes, everything can be set up just right but it does not mean everything will be successful. There are the times when one must persevere. All lines can be clean, untangled, the weather perfect, all hooks sharp and baited with the best baits, and sometimes the fish just won't bite. As in life and work, you could have or think everything is perfect, but success may elude you. During those times when you don't have success, you must continue fishing. Do what needs to be done and keep baiting the hooks. Keep running your lines. The fish will get hungry again, and you will be ready for the catch. Work hard and keep doing what is right. The old saying

that "hard work makes good luck" is true. *Do not give up.*

Align all your assets to be the most productive. Place

all your workers in their optimal position and work hard.

Hard work makes success. Dad also used to tell us that when

working for other people, we had to make sure we were

making money for them because if we were not adding value

to their business, they would not need our services.

We fished in the summer, but we also helped build

commercial chicken houses, hog farmed one summer, and

were always hauling hay and working the tobacco patches.

We added value to others' businesses to help them be

successful. Give the most of yourself so that you and others

can be successful. Be the best you can be.

And as Winston Churchill said, "Never, Never, Never, Give Up."

You Better Watch Out for the Barges

There are many things that come around in life and business that one cannot control, but we should be aware of our surroundings. As simple as it may seem sometimes there is that "big gorilla" or "elephant in the room" that folks just don't see, recognize, or acknowledge. That big gorilla could be in fishing terms, a barge, in a preacher's term, dissatisfied members, in an organization, a disgruntled employee, an up and coming competitor, or a change in technology. The term often used is "The Black Swan." This is the term for the one thing you did not think could exist or would happen until it does and then you look back and are not surprised and rationalize why it happened. To lead an organization, family, or business, one must watch out for all the hazards around you. Unlike being in a fog that may come and go as the weather changes and be short in duration and cause small impacts, the barges on the river should be seen from a great distance and they can have lasting devastating effects.

I remember our experiences on the river with a fourteen foot Jon boat and six horsepower motor. The boat and motor were small and very slow. Dad always warned us to watch out for barges and big yacht boats because their wake could swamp our little Jon boat. Dad would say, "May a word to the wise be sufficient," which is a loose quote from the book of Proverbs.

We watched on the river, as we could not necessarily hear all the hazards, but watched, as we baited our trotlines. Yes, we could get wrapped up in what we were doing and be in a world all by ourselves, grabbing the bait and intently watching the hook as we bait to insure we did not hook ourselves. We could be in a world of our own with thoughts of fishing, or dreaming of the young girls at church, but we were warned to watch out for the barges. Look up from of your work! Look up from of your life! Escape out of your body and look down at your situation. What is the barge in *your* life? What is the big gorilla in the room? What is the next Black Swan?

The barges and yachts were not only huge but would throw out gigantic waves or wakes. Two dangers existed: the size of the boats and the impact of the coming waves. Remember, even if you think the hazard is gone, you still must be alert to what could be next, what you may not be able to see or hear. The second hazard could capsize your vessel, your company, your life. You must think about the unknown possibilities and plan around the hazards of life.

Who would have thought that technology would have changed so rapidly? The story is often told on the U.S.

Patent Office that the director said in the 1800s that all that could be invented had been invented. Now we are talking about 3D printing of cars and human organs. What's next?

Be prepared, look around, and make sure you get out of the way of the barges and their waves. Remember, you may be in a small, slow Jon boat on the massive river of life.

Don't Get Lost in the Fog

You have probably heard the saying, "You can't see the forest for the trees." Well, in the fishing business we like to say, "Don't get lost in the fog." Two very similar phases which in simple terms means we often get consumed by what we perceive as all the problems. We misinterpret the situation and maybe even miss simple solutions to either simple or complex problems. We often lose focus of what our mission or purpose is as we travel the road of life.

As summer began a few years ago, I started to prepare for a little recreation. We had purchased a used jet ski two seasons prior. We previously had the opportunity to burn just a tank or two of fuel in the ski. With it still parked for winter in the basement garage, I checked the hours it had been used. The log registered 28 hours, and we had probably put on just half of those hours. I pushed the start button. and it fired right up. I then had my daughter join me as I trailered the Jet Ski to a boat ramp nearby. My daughter, Madison hopped on the Jet Ski and headed to the house as I drove the truck back home. I met her at our dock and she said it was not running at full power; it was traveling at about 24 mph instead of topping out at 55 mph. I got on the Jet Ski and experienced the same. The Jet Ski was needing some fuel, so I filled it up with about 10 gallons of gas. Our hope was the old fuel would blend in with the new fuel and our Jet Ski would be running like new again. The red and white Jet Ski looked brand new, and now we hoped it would run the same way. Madison then took the Jet Ski out and about two hours later, I received a call that she was stranded and the Jet Ski would not start. The Jet Ski was pulled home and a friend said that he thought the battery was probably dead. It was now dark, so I took a landscaping solar light and headed on to the dock to remove the battery. Back at the house I placed the battery on the charger, something I should have done prior to putting the Jet Ski in the water in the first place. Mistake number one – I got in a hurry and did not fully prepare the ski for the summer.

The battery charged overnight and the next afternoon I reinstalled the battery on the Jet Ski. With the key in the ignition I tried to start it with no success. The engine would beep, but the engine would not turn over. I returned to examine the battery. I took the key out and reentered the key a number of times, still nothing. My wife, daughter, and I then pulled the Jet Ski with my 14-foot Jon boat to the boat ramp, put the ski back on the trailer, and then back to the house. Then I decided I would take the Jet Ski to a local service center the next morning on the way to work. I was frustrated and trying not to show my emotions. I was ready to sell the Jet Ski before and even more so now. We had it for two full seasons and started the third and I did not see us getting much use of the expensive toy. The next morning I started to work towing the Jet Ski. After about three miles up the road, the fog in my brain cleared.

I pulled over, got out of my truck, inserted the dead man switch and inserted the key. The Jet Ski started right up. Mistake two was not inserting the dead man switch. Frustration was caused by not focusing on the entire situation and not having enough experience and knowledge of the equipment. Lesson learned. As I became more detached from the situation and reexamined the events, the solution became clear. Madison could not start the Jet Ski on the lake, and I could not start it on the dock because we had forgotten to reinsert the deadman's key. The sluggish machine has another safety button to be used if younger children would be driving the ski. There are often simple solutions to simple problems that we make complex.

This seems too simple and maybe one may not think it's possible in an organization or individual lives that one cannot see "the forest for the trees" or "one gets lost in the fog"; however these "lost in the fog" situations happen more often and on a much bigger scale than one might think.

The year was 1979, and an event happened which would change an industry for decades and probably forever. I was a senior in high school and was on our senior trip to Washington D. C. and New York City. While in New York a group of us 18 year olds saw a movie, "The China Syndrome." The movie depicted an event that partially became reality days later. On Tuesday, March 28, 1979, an accident occurred at the Three Mile Island (TMI) nuclear power plant in the middle of the Susquehanna River in central

Pennsylvania. The events leading up to the accident and days

later changed the nuclear power industry. That morning,

vital cooling water began escaping through an open valve in

the newer of two nuclear reactors. Dick Thornburgh,

Attorney General of the United States who spoke at the

National Press Club in Washington, D.C., some ten years later

stated, "For the next two-and-a quarter hours, plant

operators failed to read these symptoms correctly, failed to

close that valve, and mistakenly shut off an emergency

cooling system that otherwise would have operated

automatically." *Plant operators got lost in the fog.* They had

gotten too focused on one issue and they did not see the

entire operational system or possible solutions to their

problems. The Nuclear Regulatory Commission took a

proactive approach by establishing additional protocols for nuclear plant operators to help alleviate future issues.

Attorney General Thornburgh, eight months after TMI, visited the Soviet Union to share lessons learned. Thornburg's told the National Press Club, "To our discomfort, they told our party that they regarded nuclear safety as a 'solved problem,' saying that the Soviet reactors 'would soon be so safe as to be installed in Red Square' ". The Chernobyl catastrophic nuclear accident occurred in April 1986, seven years after TMI and six years after Attorney General Thornburgh shared a lesson learned.

Don't be too sure of yourself or over confident and *Don't Get Lost in the Fog*.

A Half is not a Half if it is only a Quarter – You Better Learn to Understand Some Simple Math

I heard one time that over 50% of the United States citizens do not understand fractions or decimals. In case you are one of those 50% that may not understand that 50% is also ½, one-half, 0.50, this is all simple math.

My oldest brother Brice and I worked with Dad starting at about the age of 10 and 11. We could not pull an equal weight with Dad, of course, but we were learning, trying, working, and getting prepared to one day be partners. During these younger years Dad would give us a little spending money to teach us the importance of money and more importantly, the work ethics needed to earn our way.

At the ages of about 13 and 14, Dad offered us equal partnership—or at least Dad said, "We will be equal partners." We were excited. Dad said we would share equally. At the end of the first month payday, I recall how the money was divided. Dad got one dollar, Brice got one dollar. Dad got one dollar and I got one dollar. I now remember an old Saturday cartoon when the characters were dividing up gold coins and the person counting out the coins would say, "You get one and I get one," but then would give the other character one, while the counter would take another one. The counter always had twice the stack of the others. I think Dad must have seen and learned from the cartoon.

We were getting paid fairly but things were not equal. Brother Brice and I together made up one-half which was one-quarter of the business and Dad kept the other half. Years later we became equal partners with each getting a third. This might be hard math for some but you better learn some simple math because if you don't, you will find your stack of gold from selling the fish will be ¼, one fourth, or one quarter the size of the total profits when it should have been one third.

This inspired me to become a college finance major and eventually a CPA. Learn to earn money but also learn to count it, and even more importantly, *learn how to manage it.*

Dad used to say, "It's not how much you make that is important; it's how you use what you make that's important."

Fishing on Your Way to another Job

If you are young, don't be satisfied with where you are, but work hard until you get to be where you want to be. Do what you know but continue to learn to know more and go on to bigger and greater things.

My dad was a high school teacher and in the summer catfished commercially, a skill he learned from his uncles Fred and Charlie Keylon. The art of catfishing helped feed and clothe the family by supplementing his income. Along with catfishing in the summer, Dad also lifeguarded at Camp John Knox, a Presbyterian Church camp on the Tennessee River. Dad had not studied Frederick Taylor and Frank and Lillian Gilbreth's time and motion theories, but sometimes efficiency should be just common sense. Dad's work ethics, drive, skills, and talents were put to use in the summer by getting up early to run his lines from the house along the river to Camp John Knox. He would bait the lines in the morning, lifeguard, and then have lines full of fish on his way home that afternoon. Efficiency makes successes.

Dad also was and is frugal with his money, a lesson I learned but have not practiced as well as Dad. I have often shared with students and younger employees this rule that I have practiced: Live your life on earnings from your primary job; get ahead of others and become more successful with the second job. Take the money from the second job and make your investments in real estate, stocks, and your small business. One could also say that the second job is your overtime. Don't spend your overtime earnings. Don't change your standard of living based on the second job or overtime as both can, and often do, go away.

It's your second job that will get you ahead, so Dad

had three: teaching, lifeguarding, fishing, and later in life,

cutting wood and hauling mulch. Do what it takes and work

where you are until you get to where you want to be then

work there until you get somewhere else. Dad ended his

professional career as a high school principal, and after

retiring became the principal of a local sawmill, a profession

he started working as a young man. His dad, Frank, owned a

sawmill, and that's a whole other story.

Chicken Theory

Picking on the worse performer.

I will take a break from the catfishing metaphors to talk briefly about what I learned while doing other work between fishing. Yes, fishing was work but all work was not fishing. A couple of summers between fishing, I spent time building commercial chicken houses. One summer we built new houses and the next summer we expanded a farmer's existing houses. That said, here is what I learned building and watching commercial chicken farming operations.

The weakest chicken will always get picked on by the other chickens. As I have managed and studied management over the years, I have determined that the same process happens in the office environment as it does in the chicken house. Most every chicken will pick on the weakest chicken until that chicken is dead and gone, and then the next weakest chicken becomes the target. Think about this chicken theory.

There is always that weakest chicken or employee. Never be that chicken. If you identify the weakest chicken, what should you do? Remember there will always be the weakest. Never be the weakest, but don't pick on the weakest because once the weakest is gone, the organization, I mean chicken family, will look and find the next weakest chicken. Could the weakest chicken ever be you?

I am maybe stretching the theory a little, but I see the chicken theory as having played out with Adolf Hitler in Nazi Germany. Martin Niemoller, an outspoken Protestant pastor, is remembered for this quote, which is prominently displayed in the United States Holocaust Memorial Museum:

"First they came for the Socialist and I did not speak out—

Because I was not a Socialist.

Then they came for the Trade Unionists, and I did not speak

out—

Because I was not a Trade Unionist.

Then they came for the Jews, and I did not speak out—

Because I was not a Jew.

Then they came for me—

And there was no one left to speak for me."

"Moving the Ladder Boss"

Hugh Brodgan had to have been in his mid-sixties when he worked for Gene Gamble of Gamble Home Builders. Gamble Home Builders consisted of Gene's father, Roscoe, a pastor of Chapman's Grove Baptist Church, and occasionally Gene's younger brother Bug. On two different summers, Gene picked up a few catfishermen to help build not personal homes, but chicken homes or houses. Gene was the primary owner of the family business and should have at least for those two summers changed the name of the business to the Gamble Chicken Home Builders.

Anyway, the lesson learned working with the Gamble Home Builders was learned about Hugh and how Hugh worked and what he did. Hugh at best functioned at a fifth or sixth grade level. Gene helped Hugh function in life by giving him a purpose, income, and also assisted Hugh in day to day decisions. But here is what Hugh taught us. As we were building the chicken houses, Hugh would get our tools, nails, and would move our ladders as we slid along the top of the side walls and added rafters or moved from truss to truss. Hugh would say, "Moving the Ladder, Boss." Hugh let us know what he was doing, and he did it well. He added value to the Gene Gamble Home Builders. Often times you need to let your boss know what you are doing and that you are adding value to the business. Always, "Be Moving the Ladder, Boss." You can learn from anyone.

UP

What makes success? Probably the simple words shared by others are: Get up, Dress up, Show up, Follow up, Shut up, and Never give up.

Get up—Get up and be on time. You would be surprised how most managers will judge and grade your performance on whether you are on time. It is disrespectful if the manager has to wait on you. Be there early and when there early, have something to do; read, work on a project, plan your day and your future.

Dress up—Dress appropriately for the job. Even when fishing we had a certain type of clothing we would wear. We would get cold only once a season and then we would know what to wear the next time. Late spring was warm but when the sun went down it would turn cold quickly. Shoes were important because we had to manage around hooks and catfish fins. If your job requires a suit, you had better be in a suit. If you are in a No Tattoo environment, you had better cover them up. Suit up, you are competing with others, put on your best, be presentable!

Follow up—Whatever you are working on, follow up on the task. Follow up after a job interview or a client presentation. Show others that the project and person are important to you. Projects that are important to you need to be important to them. In one of my first jobs after college, I worked with Rust Engineering and Construction Company. Our site had over 2,000 workers. I was part of a team of six whose responsibilities were to expedite materials, blueprints, and quality assurance certificates. Sometimes we even had to expedite our engineers and purchasing agents. Our job was to insure promised delivery of the right materials, on time and at the right location. I learned at Rust the importance of follow up. With material orders being three to five layers deep into a supply chain, we discovered that with numerous communication layers our "orders promised" delivery would slip, orders would be of the wrong type, kind, size, and color, or without proper certifications. The initial phone call, the follow up calls, and the occasional trip to the factory set the tone that our orders were important and we would make sure we had the correct supplies on time. Our orders were important to us, and we made sure they would be important to others by following up. Gantt chart a project but follow up on the task.

Shut up—We did not always agree with Dad. We may even have questioned him on occasion, but we also knew our limits. Sometimes the best answer and solution is to just shut up. Ask yourself if the argument with your boss,

spouse, brother or sister is that important. Just shut up.

"He who fights and walks away

Has an opportunity to fight another day.

He who fights and is slain,

Will never fight again." Unknown

"**Never Give Up**" one of Winston Churchill's greatest

speeches. - Enough said, persevere.

Trophies as Anchors

Dad was a high school principal and a highly successful girls' basketball coach. Being a successful coach meant that the school had a number of trophy cases filled with trophies from district, regional, and other tournament wins. Being a principal meant that he made decisions about how to display the many trophies the school had received over the years. To add to the many girls' trophies were also many boys' trophies from basketball championship and football bowl games. These trophies were often a figurine placed on a wooden base.

Well, the story and lesson is this, use all you have while fishing or in your journey of life. Don't let what could be considered trash, left overs, or things that could be thrown out go to waste. Use all the resources you have.

57

One summer someone broke into and vandalized the high school, turning over many of the trophy cases and breaking many of the trophies and figurines. Dad took the broken figurines, which were headed to the garbage, and brought them home. The figurines were made of metal and weighed from several ounces up to a pound.

College girls' basketball Coach Jim Davis, at the time coaching at Roane State Community College and who later coached at Clemson and Tennessee Tech, was running the trotlines with Dad one afternoon. As Coach Davis and Dad ran the line, baited the hooks, and were taking the fish off the line, Coach Davis noticed that ever so often Dad would pass a line that the bottom of the line did not surface the water. Coach Davis asked what the longer line had on it that Dad did not bait. As Dad approached the next longer line he pulled the bottom of the line up to the surface to expose a trophy figurine used as an anchor to hold the line down. Dad's response to Coach Davis was, "Jim, we were so successful winning games and tournaments and had so many trophies we decided to use the trophies as trotline anchors." Dad had beaten Jim a number of times when both were high school girls' basketball coaches. Dad got a laugh out of Jim and continued to run the line.

What is the lesson here? Have fun fishing, working, living and learning. Laugh at yourself and with others. Use all you have before you throw something away, see if there is an alternative use.

Goal is to Sell Fish

We talked a lot about fishing, how to fish, what bait to use, how trotlines are made. We learned about catfishing, but the ultimate goal was not catching the fish. The goal is selling the fish. After the fish were caught, more work was in store. We had to clean them or dress them, as we would say. We had to prepare the fish to sell. The ultimate goal, after all, was selling the fish. Define *your* goals. Many people and organizations misidentify their purpose and goals. Determine your goal. Our goal was not catching fish but selling the fish. What's your goal?

Bait all the Hooks

Dad taught us work ethics. I remember at one time every employer wanted a farm worker due to their work ethics. If you have a choice, hire a farmer. A farmer is used to getting up early, working late, being respectful, and working hard. We tackled fishing with the same drive as when we worked on our farm. Dad would say, "Bait all the hooks," which was telling us in life and in our careers to do your job and finish your work assignment. Dad continues to tell us, "Do it right, do it once, you do it wrong, and we will do it all day." "What's worth doing is worth doing right." We baited all the hooks.

I was baiting a line one evening when the local Tennessee Game Warden, Bill Holiday, pulled up, turned off his motor, and began to chat with me. I continued to bait the line. I did not think twice about it. It was natural to work and talk at the same time. The old saying we had when working and talking was, "If you cannot work and talk at the same time you better quit talking."

I'm sure I may have been a little nervous at my young age of 13, but the game warden did not scare me; I had my life jacket on, and I could see Dad at a distance in his boat. At any rate, I continued to bait the line. I just wanted to finish the work. Even though I was slowly baiting and running the line, I created a further distance from the game warden. The game warden departed and stopped down river where Dad was running and baiting a line. Dad apparently stopped baiting and running the line and chatted with the game warden. The game warden commented about stopping to see me and said, "Your son kept on baiting the line."

Don't get distracted. Don't let other things in life keep you from doing your job, even if it's the game warden. If you are doing what is right, no one can stop you.

To ensure we were doing our job, baiting all the hooks, we rotated which lines we fished. I did not know till later in my CPA career that Dad was teaching us a checks and balance system. "Trust but verify" was a famous quote by former President Ronald Reagan. Dad trusted us but also verified our work. In an accounting profession, to prevent fraud you take away the opportunity and you verify the internal control systems. You keep the honest honest by installing a checks and balances system.

Checks and balances are important and maybe even more so in the family businesses. Someone is always watching, so bait all the hooks. Do all your work. Dad said, "Do it right, do it once, do it wrong, we will do it all day."

Change as the Market Changes

Our fishing business changed over the years, and we changed with it. It was our willingness to accept change that allowed the business to continue. One may not think there would be much change in the fishing business like one may not think the same about their respective business. You must keep your eyes open, your mind open, and your ears open as change will continue to exist all around us.

In 2002, a couple of buddies of mine and I formed a partnership to purchase a 57 acre tract of land. After purchasing the property, we then hired a heavy equipment operator to clean and clear up the property. Dad saw what we were doing and commented that we were wasting our money. I said, "Dad, you must give the customer what the customer wants and most land buyers can't see the vision of

64

the value of the property until they see the property cleaned up and cleared off."

I asked, "Dad, how did we sell our catfish when we first started in the business?" He said, "Mostly live," and then I asked, "How did we sell them later?" He said, "Cleaned and dressed out but the bones were still in the fish." I said, "Then the customer wanted them filleted?" Dad said, "Yes," I said, "Next you will be cooking them." Dad looked at me and said, "You know, I have more fish fries now than I have ever had." My partners and I sold our cleaned up property.

We must change with the market to meet the customer's needs.

Don't Get Locked in the Fish Box

A fish box is a homemade box made of rough cut lumber and chicken wire. The box would be about a five foot cube. The bottom of the box would be wooden slatted, which rested at the bottom of the lake; the top would also be wooden slatted with a hinged top and latch. The sides would be wrapped in chicken wire. The fish box tied to the dock was used to place our morning catch of fish or if we only had caught a few that day, it would be a place to house the fish until we had sufficient fish to clean.

In the winter time, the Tennessee Valley Authority, which managed the Tennessee River for flood control, would lower the lake level. The cove we lived in would become a mud flat, and the fish box would be resting on dry land or mud. We could walk where the water once was, and we would play on the dry lake bottom.

It was Christmas and family time with our first cousins visiting from various parts of Tennessee. We always would come together at Christmas each year. Our moms and dads would stay in the house and talk about the old days and the younger cousins were creating memories as we would talk about days into the future. Christmas times today, we still get together and we always talk about a trip to New Orleans where Randall was shot, and we talk about the time we locked Jeff in the fish box.

All the cousins were playing near the dock on the mud flat beside the empty fish box. Yes, the older cousins talked our younger cousin, Jeff, into getting into the fish box, at which point we locked the hatch. Jeff was locked in the fish box. Jeff is now a professional therapist. We attribute

Jeff's success to those experiences of his youth given to him

by his older cousins. It might be those experiences of youth

that set our career paths. I'm sure Jeff shares this experience

with his clients, and we share it with each other every

Christmas. The experiences of your youth help make you

who you are, and some of these experiences you enjoy again

and again. My advice is be aware of your surroundings and

who you trust. You may not be able to trust your favorite

cousins, who might just lock you in the fish box.

A Fish Rots from the Head First

We caught and cleaned many fish in our years on the lake. We had galvanized wash tubs and five gallon plastic buckets in the Jon boats to put our fish in as we would take them off the lines. We also put the remains of fish after we cleaned them in the buckets to feed the turtles of the cove. We had a fish box tied to the docks to house our fish until we had enough to clean. On occasion, a fish would die before cleaning, and we would discard the entire fish. The dead fish may have died on the trotline, in the wash tub, or even in the fish box. We would put the dead fish in the five gallon bucket and set the bucket in the boat waiting until the next time we went to run a trotline, and then we would discard the dead fish. A dead fish would often stay in the bucket from morning to evening. The lesson we learned was that a fish rots from the head first. Just like an organization dies and lives based on the capability of the head of the organization, so does a catfish. In the long term, an organization succeeds or fails based on the head of the organization. We all have seen an organization with a bad leader be successful, but it is generally for only a short time. A weak or bad leader will negatively impact a successful and productive culture and organization and sooner or later will turn the successful organization to a failed organization. This is very simple. A fish rots from the head first, and so does any organization, period!

Staff Meeting a Necessary Evil

Believe it or not, even in a two-boat 13-trotline family business, we had staff meetings. I've been working over 30 years and have always been with organizations that had the dreaded staff meetings.

Necessary evils, I would call them, and I have called many meetings myself. Staff meetings are established for communication and keeping our projects on track.

The Woody's two-boat 13-trotline family business had a staff meeting each morning, where we received our daily orders for fishing, farming, mowing the yard, or whatever Dad needed to share with the boys. Mom called it breakfast.

Know Your Limitations

We fished from the signal light at Tennessee River mile marker 558.2 down to Thief Neck Island signal light 556. Never at any point in time did we have lines at the exterior points at the same time. We kept our lines within a narrow area. We had two boats powered by 6 horsepower Johnsons. We knew the distances we could efficiently fish. Our house was positioned about the midpoint between Thief Neck and the signal light marker 558.2. We lived on the east side of the Tennessee River.

What we learned with our 6 HP motors is that one must know their limitations as in business or life. We were only limited on the horse power, as we knew the river quite well and had frequently travelled outside what we defined as our fishing zone. We knew fish were in all parts of the river, but to be effective we knew the scope of what was most

efficient and we stayed with it. We did what was successful

and we did it well. Know your limitations.

Signals and Navigations

As mentioned previously, our house was positioned between one defined light signal on Thief Neck Island and a blinking light up river. All day these lights would blink and go unnoticed by the boaters. One never saw the blinking lights during the day. Neither did anyone notice during the day signal light located on the banks of the islands. But at night, the lights guided the barges and other commercial or overnight recreation travelers. We seldom night fished or travelled the river at night. but when we did, the lights were our salvation, showing us home and giving us peace of mind. It is so easy to get lost in the fog and at night without a clear and well-lit sky or the blinking navigation lights. Today our boats have navigational and GPS systems, and the Tennessee River navigation signal lights are no longer maintained. But the lights of times past allowed us to keep in the main channel out of the hazards of shallow water. The lights continued to blink as you traveled up or down the river. One could line your boat between the light in front and the light behind with confidence you were always in the main channel. As you approached the light in front, you would be continually looking for the next light in front, and as soon as you saw that light, you would turn your boat to the direction of the farther light in front of you. You always were looking ahead to the next light in your direction of travel. Occasionally, you would have to look back to make sure your boat was lined up between the back and front blinking lights.

All organizations and families have rules of navigation. One needs to know the rules and abide by the rules and, like being on the river with the signal lights no longer being maintained, the rules change. Change with the rules as they change.

The river had the night navigation lights but also had buoys you could see during the day, which also reflected at night when your boat lights or flashlight shown on the buoys. Keep your boat to the right of the green buoys going upstream and to the left of the red buoys. The seaman's saying is, "Red Right Return." Going upstream to the higher mile markers, you are returning, and you kept the Red Buoys to your Right. I generally would get confused so it became just common sense time, stay between the buoys and generally on most days you could see both the green and red buoys, but at night you learned to travel a little slower even with a 6HP Johnson to get your bearings of the buoy locations.

We seldom fished in the main channel, nor did we travel the main channel, but that was because we knew the river and the hazards outside the channel. Learning the hazards consisted of trial and error, reading navigation maps, studying the water's movement, and observing the water's clarity. In organizations, some rules are written, like the river navigation maps, lights, and buoys, but more important are the unwritten rules of conduct. Always be on the safe side and obey the navigational rules, understanding the safety of the main channel but also being aware that outside the main channel are the most important rules, which are the unwritten rules of the organization. Be cautious in these hazardous waters.

A Methodist Dozen

"Make money from your friends because your
enemies will not trade with you." - unknown

Your best customers are your repeat customers.
Businesses often calculate how much money it costs to
obtain new customers, but one seldom sees studies of the
cost of maintaining the existing customer. Existing customers
are the most important customers to your organization.
Satisfied customers are your repeat customers, but also the
best marketing tool for your new customers.

We caught and cleaned the fish, but it was Mom who
put the final touches on the finished product. Our workday
would be over, but Mom did the final cleaning, packaging,
labeling, and loving touch and her work would just be

beginning . The fish were rinsed and rinsed repeatedly, making the fish white and tasty. Excess skin and fat were trimmed off.   The fish were rinsed again, weighed, and readied for packaging. When Mom weighed the fish, she would always put a little extra weight in from what would be listed on the label. Mom called it a little Methodist dozen (13 made a dozen instead of 12). Give the customer a great product and more than they expected. Not only will they come back, but they will bring other customers.

Remember your customers are your friends, so be nice, polite, and fair, and help your customers to be satisfied. You must remember you make money from your friends because your enemies will not trade with you.

Trotline, Jug, Pole Fishing

We mainly trotline fished, but on occasion, we also jugged and pole fished. Jug fishing. or some refer to it as noodle fishing, again a change in fishing technology, means a change in name. You better get used to change.   Change is inevitable and has always happened and will always happen. Anyway back to jug/noodle fishing: a trotline nylon string from three (3) to six (6) feet in length is tied to a floater object (jug or noodle) and at the other end place two hooks about a foot apart and maybe a small weight of a few ounces. To jug fish, one needs a calm day so the jugs will not blow with the wind. One would also fish with up to 30 jugs. Hopefully you understand now why the wind must be calm; chasing 30 jugs with a wind would be enough work itself.

Jugs are placed in a cove anywhere from 10 feet to 20 feet apart and water depth from 5 to 15 feet. It is not uncommon that before you have all the jugs baited and placed in the cove, you will be seeing one or two on the run or bobbing up and down. You can stay busy for an hour or two running the jugs and catching the fish. Jug fishing is fun, and you have immediate gratification of your work; when your jugs are moving you know you have a good catch. Positive feedback is important and improves performance because you see you are catching fish. Jug fishing took place during the day, and at night we would pole fish, baiting with red worms or pieces of hot dogs. We would tie our poles to the dock or rest the pole on a fork branch and sit and watch the poles. We each would also fish with more than one pole.

Do what you have to do to be successful and learn other compatible skills because you never know what skills you may need and the more you have, the more valuable you become.

As in trot lining, jug, or pole fishing, do what you must to be successful. Get the job accomplished and do what you do best.

Our Decisions Were Simple

Life got more complicated after fishing. Looking back, "those were the days." Mom made breakfast, lunch, and dinner. Brice and I were in our early teens and had our own boat and partial freedom on the water. Dad gave us our instructions for the day. We did not have to make many decisions, and the ones we made were simple. What to wear, what row in the garden we were going to hoe or how fast to hoe it or how we were going to mow the yard or who was going to bait the first trotline. Those were simple times. We moved on. Then younger brothers Randall and Preston became partners with Dad, and Brice and I started another life. Brice went to technical school to become a welder, and I attended a community college and on to receive a finance degree. Randall and Preston would move on, and Dad would end up fishing the way he began, by himself.

Fishing is a simple life that Dad still enjoys at 80, simpler than his days as a high school principal. From the simple times and simple decisions, I married, becoming a father with a son and a daughter. Seems as life goes on, decisions become more difficult, but one thing I learned over time with my experience was to make decisions on facts, analysis, and study. All decisions will not be correct, but the odds improve when you analyze the facts and situations.

The father of the Nuclear Navy, Admiral Hyman Rickover, had stringent standards and a powerful focus on achievement. He was known to write it down. Write down the problems, the facts, and what you are trying to accomplish meant writing things down which helps us focus and clarify the situation. An unknown quote I have often used summarizes the important of writing down facts and goals: "Framing the issue may be the most important thing we do, for how we define the problems help determine what we do to solve them."

"Important issues should be presented in writing. Nothing so sharpens the thought process as writing down one's arguments. Weaknesses overlooked in oral discussion become painfully obvious on the written page." Admiral H.G. Rickover- "Father of the Nuclear Navy"- excerpt from 1982 Columbia University speech.

Fishing is simple, Life is complicated.

New Baits

Everyone who fishes for catfish has used red worms, but when you bait 100 hook lines with red worms, you start looking for more effective, efficient bait sources. We went to The Shipwash House Farm on Highway 58 and dug in the manure for the red worms. But we had problems with the worm bait. Worms were often hard to find in the dry summer, and it was hard to get enough to bait all the hooks. Fish other than catfish would often strip the worms off the hooks without getting caught. We also would catch crawfish for bait and like worms, we would count them, ensuring we had enough to bait all the hooks. A good thing about the crawfish was that they would stay on the hooks alive until eaten, which allowed us to run a line without having to bait all the hooks.

At certain times of the year, we were climbing trees and counting the catalpa worms, shaking the trees, and the worms would fall to the ground. Our baits got easier and better over time, just like a business should. We, just like any employee, were learning more and putting what we learned to use. The next bait was shad minnows. You can catch them with a cast net, and if you found a good school of the minnows you could get enough in a cast for a trotline or two. Within minutes instead of hours you could have all the bait you needed. Yes, easy, but also an effective bait. Every now and then you would get a big shad fish that would become cut bait. Not as good as the minnow bait, but it would stay on the hooks for days when the minnows would be off in 24 hours. Different times of the spring and summer brought us different baits. The crawfish were used in the spring and summer. The catalpa worms were used in the early summer, and shad minnows in the summer.

We then discovered Ivory Soap, simple and effective. The soap was cut in little chunks with a soap cutter. The soap kept the line clean. Dad used to tell people that the fish would come up to wash in the morning and get caught. I don't think Procter and Gamble Company ever advertised Ivory Soap as bait, but if you are baiting 1300 hooks, it is efficient and effective.

Different seasons call for different baits. We learned to use what we had until 40 years later we discovered an advancement in catfishing. It was there before us the whole time. For some 40 years for brother Brice and me and maybe 70 years for Dad, we had a bait in front of us that we did not recognize. Something new, something simple, something successful: the new bait was catfish bellies. Every time you caught and cleaned a fish, you would cut off the belly, which proved to be a convenient and efficient bait. Sometimes the solutions are right in front of us. We get lost in the forest because of the trees, or we get lost in the fog because we are not paying attention. Keep your eyes, ears, and mind open for paths to success for the new discovery may just be right in front of you.

We used the bait we had that was in season. We used what we had till we discovered something better.

Fishing is Solitude

When fishing you can find solitude. You were either with your dad creating fond memories, older brother talking about school, church, girls, friends, and other jobs for the summer, or you were fishing by yourself. Everyone will have time alone, so it's important to be able to learn to be by oneself. Throughout life there will come a time when you have solitude, either seclusion or isolation due to a failed relationship, loss of a loved one, or it could be bad chemistry at work.

What's important is how you handle that solitude. Use the time to be productive, reflective, restful, and resourceful. It's late in the evening; the sun is beginning to set; the water is calm and the air is pleasant. You feel the presence of the Almighty. You don't think about your problems. You think of all your blessings. You go over all you

should be thankful for. Value your solitude.

In Conclusion

As we go through life we can identify many metaphors that help us better understand and develop a connection with humanity and the so called "Meaning of Life and Living". Catfishing and life on the river has been one of my metaphors.

I hope this book has made you laugh a little, remember a little about the good times of your youth, and inspired you to do your best in life.

As this final chapter comes to an end, my mom, dad, brothers, cousins, and friends anticipate the soon release. They have begun to ask whether other details stories are included such as: Randall being shot in New Orleans; Preston, Bubba (my son) and I being part of a world record while sleeping in an underwater habitat in Key Largo, Florida;

my oldest cousin and son getting lost in a fog bank while trying to meet dad to the run the trotlines; the cousins gathering one Christmas and hiking to a local cave and getting lost in the cave; and if many more are in the book? I had to tell them "no". These stories have not been written yet and may have to be told another time and in another book.

But for now let's have a little peace, quiet, and solitude fishing and living on the Tennessee River.

God Bless us all.

Acknowledgements

A special thanks go out to my dad and mom, Boyd and Joyce Woody, for my childhood memories and the love they gave my brothers and me.

To the characters in the book, you all made for interesting stories and taught me much about life for that and more I'm forever grateful. Thanks for the memories.

Editors of Rosemary Alexander, BJ Gillum, Mom, and Pastor Chuck Griffin, I know you all struggled through my manuscripts for which I'm most grateful.

Thanks, Jasmine DeGroot for editing and formatting the book.

To my wife, Becky, for understanding my sleepless nights as I had to write while things were on my mind.

Finally and most important, I thank God for His Blessing and as Thomas Dorsey wrote after the death of his wife and infant daughter, "Precious, Lord Take My Hand."

Made in the USA
San Bernardino, CA
09 July 2016